EVALUATING SOFTWARE COMPLEXITY MEASURES

Elaine J Weyuker

Department of Computer Science
Courant Institute of Mathematical Sciences
New York University
251 Mercer Street
New York, New York 10012

ABSTRACT

A set of properties of syntactic software complexity measures is proposed to serve as a basis for the evaluation of such measures Four well-known complexity measures are evaluated and compared using these criteria This type of formalized evaluation should help to clarify the strengths and weaknesses of proposed complexity measures, and ultimately lead to the definition of better measures by emphasizing important properties

KEY WORDS Software complexity, software metrics, software science, data flow, cyclomatic number

January 1985

EVALUATING SOFTWARE COMPLEXITY MEASURES

Elaine J. Weyuker

INTRODUCTION

In the last several years, there has been a great deal of interest in defining appropriate ways to measure the complexity of software. Most of the proposed measures are syntactic in nature and frequently involve counting one or more textual property of the program. In most cases, the author presents arguments to show that as the frequency of the selected feature increases, while everything else remains the same, so does the complexity of the program. What is generally not investigated is whether the selected features are the *only* ones which affect complexity.

Rather than informally discussing the pros and cons of various proposed measures, or doing an empirical study to see how well each of the proposed measures correlate with actual data, we present instead abstract properties that permit us to formally compare software complexity models. This should allow one to determine the most suitable measure for various purposes and to evaluate newly proposed measures. We then check whether or not such well-known complexity measures as cyclomatic number, Halstead's programming effort, statement count, and Oviedo's data flow complexity satisfy our properties.

Similar attempts to abstract desirable properties of software metrics, and thereby facilitate the comparison and evaluation of competing models have recently been reported. Weyuker [26] has looked at properties of software test data adequacy criteria, and Iannino et al [11] have done similar research for software reliability models.

One of the difficulties in assessing complexity measures is that it is not always clear what the measure is supposed to be measuring. Frequently mentioned characteristics include the difficulty of implementing, testing, understanding, modifying, or maintaining a program. But in most cases, these terms are themselves vague. By formalizing the properties we used for evaluation, measures can be compared and assessed based on the particular needs of the user of the proposed metric

DEFINITIONS

Although most of the ideas of the paper are not really dependent on the particular details of the programming language, it is nonetheless necessary to have an explicit syntax in order to make our definitions precise. Our language will contain a finite number of identifiers. *Arithmetic expressions* are to be constructed using constants, identifiers, and the arithmetic operators $+$, $-$, $*$, $/$, in the usual manner.

An *assignment statement* has the form:

$$VAR \leftarrow EXP$$

where VAR is an identifier and EXP is an arithmetic expression.

A *predicate* is a Boolean expression having one of the forms

$$B1 = B2, \ B1 \neq B2, \ B1 < B2, \ B1 \leq B2,$$

where B1 and B2 are each either a constant or an identifier. A *program body* is defined recursively

(1) An assignment statement is a program body

(2) IF PRED THEN P
        ELSE Q
        END
is a program body if PRED is a predicate and P and Q are program bodies

(3) IF PRED THEN P END
is a program body if PRED is a predicate and P is a program body

(4) WHILE PRED DO P
        ENDWHILE
is a program body if PRED is a predicate and P is a program body

(5) P
   Q
is a program body if P and Q are program bodies

We shall refer to program bodies of the form (2), (3), or (4) as *conditionals*

A *program statement* has the form

PROGRAM(variables)

where variables is a list of the input variables

An *output statement* has the form

OUTPUT(variables)

where variables is a list of the output variables

Finally, a *program* consists of a **PROGRAM** statement, followed by a program body, followed by an **OUTPUT** statement We will frequently call this program body a program, provided no confusion results Since our language consists of entirely familiar locutions, there is no need for us to specify further its formal semantics.

For a given program P, we write $P(c) = b$ to mean that the program P on input c halts with output b We write $P \equiv Q$ (P is *equivalent to* Q), to mean that $P(c) = Q(c)$ for every input c

Oviedo's [18] definitions of some of the terms needed to describe his complexity measure differ somewhat from other's use of the same terms [9, 22] We therefore present his definitions

A *program block* is a **PROGRAM** statement, an **OUTPUT** statement, a predicate with its associated keywords (i e **IF PRED**, **WHILE PRED DO**), or a group of sequentially executed statements defined as follows

A statement "A" is a block entry if it is the first statement after the **PROGRAM** statement, or it is a **THEN** statement, or an **ELSE** statement, or a statement which can be reached from two or more blocks (e g a statement following a conditional) or a statement which can be executed immediately after a **WHILE PRED DO** block

The block belonging to a block entry "A" consists of "A" and all the statements following "A" up to and including either an **ENDWHILE** statement, or a statement which is immediately followed by a block entry or program block

A *program flow graph* is a directed graph in which each node corresponds to a block of the program and the edges correspond to the program branches. If the nodes n_i and n_j of the flow graph correspond to the program blocks n_i and n_j then there is an edge (n_i,n_j) from node n_i to node n_j if it is possible for control to transfer from block n_i to block n_j in the program

One way to think of a program is as an object made up of smaller programs. Certainly this is the perspective used in our definition of a program body, or any recursive definition. Using this point of view, the basic operation in constructing programs is composition. Since each of the programming language constructs is single entry and single exit, it makes sense to speak of concatenating two program bodies P,Q is the program body formed by appending the program body Q immediately following the last statement of P We shall say that P,Q is *composed from* P and Q Because of this perspective, we will apply measures of complexity to program bodies, rather than programs This will not affect the results in any substantial way for any of the measures considered

In the sequel, P, Q, and R will denote program bodies, and $|P|$ will denote the complexity of P, with respect to some hypothetical measure We shall assume that for any complexity measure being considered and any program body P, $|P|$ is a non-negative number It follows immediately, therefore, that for any P and Q,

$$|P| \leq |Q| \quad \text{or} \quad |Q| \leq |P|$$

That is, the complexity of any pair of program bodies can be compared and ordered.

Using this perspective that programs are composed from smaller programs, a fundamental question is Given two programs which are related by composition, should their complexities be related? We will discuss this and similar questions, and examine various complexity measures in terms of these questions

COMPLEXITY MEASURES

A large number of software complexity measures have been proposed in recent years, and there have been a number of interesting comparisons of the usefulness of these complexity measures [1, 3, 4, 13, 23, 27]. Among the most frequently cited measures are the number of program statements, McCabe's cyclomatic number [15] Halstead's programming effort [6], and the knot measure [28] We will not consider this last measure, since for a structured language such as ours, the knot measure of every program is 0

Probably the oldest and most intuitively obvious notion of complexity is the number of statements in the program, or the *statement count* A primary advantage of this measure is its simplicity, however one chooses to define a statement, (and in particular how compound statements are counted) it is a straight-forward and easily automated task to compute the statement complexity of a program

McCabe [15] defines the complexity of a program to be

$$v = e - n + 2p$$

where e is the number of edges in a program flow graph, n the number of nodes, and p the number of connected components It is further demonstrated that if p=1, then $v = \pi + 1$ where π is the number of predicates in the program.

Questions have been raised as to the most appropriate way to treat compound predicates [16], but once that decision has been made, the cyclomatic complexity of a single component program is trivial to compute Since our programming language permits only simple predicates, this question is moot for us

Halstead [6] introduced software science in an attempt to measure properties of programs Following Halstead's notation

$$\eta_1 = \text{number of distinct operators}$$
$$\eta_2 = \text{number of distinct operands}$$
$$N = \text{total number of operators}$$

$$N_2 = \text{total number of operands}$$

The program volume is defined to be.

$$V = (N_1 + N_2) \log_2(\eta_1 + \eta_2)$$

The potential volume, V^*, is defined as the minimum possible volume for a given algorithm Programming effort is then defined to be

$$E = V^2/V^*$$

Since V^* is obviously difficult to compute, and not a purely syntactic notion, an approximate computational formula is frequently used [3, 5, 6] as a measure of program complexity

$$E = \frac{\eta_1 N_2 (N_1 + N_2) \log_2(\eta_1 + \eta_2)}{2\eta_2}$$

This is a purely syntactic, implementation-dependent notion, and we shall refer to this measure in the sequel as the-*effort measure*. When several program bodies are being compared, we shall sometimes wish to indicate the program body for which a property is being computed Thus we shall write $E(P)$ to denote the effort for program body P or $\eta_2(Q)$ to denote the number of distinct operands in Q

A substantially different type of complexity measure, based on the data flow characteristics of a program, was proposed by Oviedo [18] The programming language he defined is similar to the one given above, although **GOTO** statements are permitted in his language but do not contribute to the data flow complexity of the program We again follow his definitions

A *variable definition* takes place in a PROGRAM statement or in an assignment statement A *variable reference* takes place when the variable is used in an expression (i e in an assignment statement or predicate) or an OUTPUT statement

A *locally available* variable definition for a program block is a definition of the variable in the block A *locally exposed* variable reference in a block is a reference to a variable which is not preceded in the block by a definition of that variable

A variable definition in block n_l is said to *reach* block n_k if the definition is locally available in block n_l and there is a path from n_l to n_k (i e n_k is a successor of n_l) along which the variable is not locally available in any block on the path   A variable definition in a block *kills* all other definitions of this variable that might otherwise reach the block   Then

$$R_l = \text{the set of variable definitions that reach } n_l$$

Oviedo makes the following assumptions

(1)   a programmer can determine the definition-reference relationships *within* blocks more easily than the definition-reference relationships *between* blocks, and

(2)   the number of different variables which are locally exposed in each block is more important than the total number of locally exposed variable references in each block

Let V_l be the set of variables whose references are locally exposed in block n_l Then block n_l's *data flow complexity* is

$$DF_l = \sum_{j=1}^{\|V_l\|} DEF(v_j)$$

where $DEF(v_j)$ represents the number of available definitions of variable v_j in the set R_l, and $\|V_l\|$ denotes the cardinality of the set V_l That is, DF_l counts all prior definitions of locally exposed variables in n_l which reach n_l

Finally, the *data flow complexity* of a program body is

$$DF = \sum_{l=1}^{\|S\|} DF_l$$

That is, the data flow complexity of a program body is the sum of the data flow complexities of each block of the program body   By this definition, only *interblock* data flow contributes to the complexity of a program body   We will write DF(P) to denote the data flow complexity of P   Since we consider the complexity of program bodies, and a variable referenced within a program body may have been defined in a different program body, we assume that for every variable referenced in the program body, there is a single definition at the entry node (i e , we assume there is a **PROGRAM** statement which defines each variable) Recall that every program body is single entrant, and hence it makes sense to speak of "the entry node".

This definition is closely related to the test data selection or adequacy criterion, *all-uses*, defined in [20, 21] which requires that a test case be included which exercises every definition-reference pair Similar testing criteria have also been proposed in [10, 14, 17] Other complexity measures have been proposed which depend at least in part on data flow in [12, 13, 24]

PROPERTIES OF THE COMPLEXITY MEASURES

We now begin our investigation of desirable properties of complexity measures All of the measures we consider, depend only on syntactic features of the program This is desirable, even necessary, as virtually all-semantic questions about a program are in general recursively undecidable [25]

Our first property is really a property of measures in general Surely, a measure which rates all programs as equally complex is not really a measure We therefore propose.

PROPERTY 1 $(\exists P)(\exists Q)(|P| \neq |Q|)$

Clearly, this is a property which is satisfied by each of the measures we consider Recall, however, that it was the failure to satisfy this property for structured languages that led us to exclude the knot metric from this study

A somewhat stronger property reflects the fact that we are considering *syntactic* complexity measures

PROPERTY 2 $(\exists P)(\exists Q)(P \equiv Q \ \& \ |P| \neq |Q|)$

The intuition behind Property 2 is that even though two programs compute the same function it is the details of the implementation that determine the program's complexity That is, we are measuring the complexity of the *program*, not the function being computed by the program Since all the measures we consider are entirely implementation dependent, they all satisfy this property

A different strengthening of Property 1 requires that the measure not be too "flat" Property 1 states that a measure should not rank all programs as equally complex Similar intuition implies that a measure is not sensitive enough if it divides all programs into just "a few" complexity classes Property 3 is an attempt to formalize this intuition In a much more abstract vein, Blum [2] presented a pair of axioms which, it is generally believed, should be satisfied by any reasonable definition of complexity Property 3 is Blum's first axiom

PROPERTY 3 Let c be a non-negative number_ Then, there are only finitely-many programs of complexity c

Our language permits only finitely-many identifiers In addition, it is reasonable to assume there is some largest possible number that can be represented and an upper bound on the length of an instruction (perhaps measured in terms of the number of bits needed to represent the instruction, or the number of operators or operands permitted, or some similar syntactically determinable characteristic) This upper bound may be a function of the particular machine used, and will be assumed to exist

With these assumptions, it follows that statement count fulfills Property 3, but cyclomatic number does not This reflects one of the obvious intuitive weaknesses of the cyclomatic number measure it makes no provision for distinguishing between programs which perform very little computation and those which perform massive amounts of computation, provided that they have the same decision structure This was, at least in part, Hansen's motivation for defining the complexity measure in [7]

Since our language permits only finitely-many identifiers and constants, there are at most finitely-many distinct operands in a program. Similarly, the language contains only a fixed, finite number of distinct operators. Therefore, for given values of η_1 and η_2, there are only finitely-many program bodies having that number of distinct operators and operands. Since $N_2(P) \geq \eta_2(P)$, it then follows that for a given value e of E, there are only finitely-many different program bodies P such that $E(P) = e$.

For data flow complexity, Property 3 does not hold, since a program body could contain arbitrarily many assignment statements of the form

$$VAR \leftarrow C$$

where VAR is an identifier and C is a constant. These statements contribute nothing to the data flow complexity of the program body. Of course, one might argue that such a counterexample of this property is not really a reasonable one, especially since there are only finitely-many identifiers and constants. But since intrablock data flow does not contribute at all to the complexity of a program body, a block could contain the statements

$$\begin{array}{l} X \leftarrow C \\ X \leftarrow f(X) \end{array}$$

$$X \leftarrow f(X)$$

where f is some function of one variable and there are arbitrarily many copies of the statement "$X \leftarrow f(X)$" in the block. These statements add nothing to the complexity opf the program body in which they appear, and thus the complexity of the program body would be the same whether there were one or one million copies of the statement.

Our view of programs is that they are objects composed from simpler programs (or more properly program bodies). Thus it is important to consider the relative complexities of program bodies related in this way. Central to any notion of syntactic program complexity, should be the property that the components of a program are no more complex than the program itself We believe that "monotonicity" is another fundamentally important property and it is difficult to imagine the sense in which a measure which fails to satisfy the monotonicity property is measuring complexity. That is

PROPERTY 4 $(\forall P)(\forall Q)(|P| \leq |P,Q| \text{ and } |Q| \leq |P,Q|)$

It is easy to see that for statement count, $(\forall P)(\forall Q)(|P,Q| = |P| + |Q|)$ and for cyclomatic number $(\forall P)(\forall Q)(|P,Q| = |P| + |Q| - 1)$ It follows immediately from these relationships that Property 4 holds for statement count and cyclomatic number It is very disappointing to discover, however, that Property 4 does not hold for data flow complexity or the effort measure

For the data flow measure, the problem arises because only *interblock* data flow contributes to the program's complexity Thus, if when P and Q are concatenated they form a single block, the complexity, as computed by this measure, could well decrease For example, the program body X - 0 has a data flow complexity of 0 while the program body Y - X has a data flow complexity of 1 The program body formed by concatenation

$$X \leftarrow 0$$
$$Y \leftarrow X$$

has a data flow complexity of 0 (since all data references are to variables defined within the block), which is less than the complexity of one of its parts

The problem appears to arise only in cases in which two program bodies (or parts of program bodies) are composed to form a single block If this is not the case, then $(\forall P)(\forall Q)(|P,Q| \geq |P| + |Q|)$, and hence Property 4 holds

For the effort measure, however, the problem seems to be far more fundamental Consider the case of a program body P with $\eta_1 = 12$, $\eta_2 = 4$, $N_1 = 35$, and $N_2 = 44$ For such a program, $E(P) = 20856$ Assume P,Q is a program body composed from (the above) P and Q with $\eta_1 = 12$, $\eta_2 = 20$, $N_1 = 40$, and $N_2 = 60$ Then $E(P,Q) = 9000$

We see that for this, and many other easily constructed cases, $E(P) > E(P,Q)$ (i e $|P| > |P,Q|$) Notice that this is a feasible set of values If P and Q use exactly the same set of operators, then $\eta_1(P) = \eta_1(Q) = \eta_1(P,Q)$ In addition, assume that each of the 4 distinct operands of P are each used 11 times, and hence $N_2(P) = 44$ If Q contains 16 distinct operands (i e $\eta_2(Q) = 16$) each used once, then $N_2(Q) = 16$ If, furthermore, the operands of P are all different from the operands of Q, it follows that $\eta_2(P,Q) = 4 + 16 = 20$, and $N_2(P,Q) = 44 + 16 = 60$

Programming effort was proposed as a measure of the amount of effort (time) needed to construct a given program It is difficult to imagine an argument that it is reasonable that it would take more effort to produce the initial portion of a program, than to produce the entire program The failure of the effort measure to fulfill this property is therefore of fundamental importance, and makes questionable its usefullness as a complexity measure

Two variants of this measure have been proposed and used [6, 29] and it is interesting to notice that this property does not hold for any of these versions of the effort measure Halstead speaks of "impurities" (which are frequently interpreted to be instances of poor programming style), and uses the following measure of effort to minimize their effects when present

$$E = \frac{\eta_1 N_2 (\eta_1 \log_2 \eta_1 + \eta_2 \log_2 \eta_2) \log_2 (\eta_1 + \eta_2)}{2\eta_2}$$

That is, the estimator $\eta_1 \log_2 \eta_1 + \eta_2 \log_2 \eta_2$ replaces $N_1 + N_2$ Using this definition of E, and the values of η_1, η_2, and N_2 for P and P,Q of the example above, it follows that

$$E(P) = 13469$$

$$E(P,Q) = 11648$$

and thus Property 4 does not hold for this version of the effort measure

A third variant of the effort measure is based on defining

$$V^* \quad (2 + \eta_2^*)\log_2(2 + \eta_2^*)$$

where η_2^* is the number of input/output operands needed by the program. Then

$$E = \frac{((N_1 + N_2)\log_2(\eta_1 + \eta_2))^2}{(2 + \eta_2^*)\log_2(2 + \eta_2^*)}$$

Considering again the above example, with $\eta_2^*(P) = 2$, and $\eta_2^*(P,Q) = 14$, for this measure of effort,

$$E(P) = 12482$$

$$E(P,Q) = 3906$$

This demonstrates that Property 4 does not hold for any of the three proposed definitions of the effort measure.

Another related question to consider is whether or not the concatenation of a given program body with other program bodies should always affect the complexity of the resultant program body in a uniform way? Although a given program body R has a fixed complexity in isolation, in some cases R may not interact at all with a program body it is concatenated with, while in other cases the two program bodies will interact in subtle and important ways which affect the complexity of the resulting program body. This is reflected in the next property.

PROPERTY 5a $(\exists P)(\exists Q)(\exists R)(|P| = |Q| \,\&\, |P,R| \neq |Q,R|)$

        b $(\exists P)(\exists Q)(\exists R)(|P| = |Q| \,\&\, |R,P| \neq |R,Q|)$

Since both cyclomatic number and statement count view program bodies as having inherent complexities which are static, regardless of their context, they are not able to reflect this possible difference in interaction, and hence neither measure satisfies Property 5.

To see that these properties hold for the data flow measure, let P be a program body using a given set of variables, while Q is a program body using a different set of variables. If R uses some of the same variables as P, then the computation in R might depend directly on the computation in P and this should be reflected in the complexity. In contrast, assume Q and R use totally disjoint sets of variables. In that case, they can be considered to call for two totally independent computations and thus Q,R might be expected to have a lower complexity than P,R A similar example can be constructed to show that Property 5b holds for data flow complexity

It is also easy to show that Property 5 holds for the effort measure Let P and Q be program bodies using exactly the same set of operators and the same total number of operators. Then $\eta_1(P)=\eta_1(Q)$ and $N_1(P)=N_1(Q)$ Assume too that P and Q have the same number of distinct operands, but that no operand is used in both P and Q (that is, the sets of operands in P and Q are disjoint), and that the total number of operands used in P and Q is the same Then $\eta_2(P)=\eta_2(Q)$ and $N_2(P)=N_2(Q)$ Therefore it follows that $E(P) = E(Q)$

Now assume that R uses exactly the same set of operators as P and Q, and the same set of operands as P (and hence a set disjoint from Q's set of operands) Then

$$\eta_1(P,R) = \eta_1(Q,R)$$
$$N_1(P;R) = N_1(Q,R)$$
$$\eta_2(P,R) = \eta_2(P)$$
$$\eta_2(Q,R) = \eta_2(Q) + \eta_2(R) = \eta_2(P) + \eta_2(R) > \eta_2(P,R)$$
$$N_2(P,R) = N_2(P) + N_2(R) = N_2(Q) + N_2(R) = N_2(Q,R)$$

Therefore, in computing the efforts for P,R and Q,R, the only different value of the factors is $\eta_2(Q,R) > \eta_2(P,R)$ Hence, $E(P,R) \neq E(Q,R)$ even though $E(P) = E(Q)$

Consider now two program bodies P and Q which contain exactly the same statements but in different orders Are P and Q always of equal complexity? We believe the answer to this question should be "not necessarily" Other researchers have argued convincingly that the order of statements may well affect the complexity Harrison and Magel [8] and Piwowarski [19] argued, for example, that the depth of nesting of loops play a critical rôle in the complexity of software For a non-structured language, Woodward et al [28] argued that the complexity of a program is determined by the flow of control through the program, and hence the order of the statements

Property 6 asserts that program complexity should be responsive to the order of the statements, and hence the potential interaction among statements

PROPERTY 6 There are program bodies P and Q such that Q is formed by permuting the order of the statements of P, and $|P| \neq |Q|$

Neither statement count, cyclomatic number, nor the effort measure, satisfy this property since the complexity of a program is completely independent of the placement, and therefore potential interaction among, the program's statements using these measures   In contrast, since the placement of statements may affect their interaction and hence the program's complexity if evaluated using the data flow measure, one would expect this property to hold

To verify that this property does indeed hold for data flow complexity, consider the following program bodies.

```
P. WHILE X≥0 DO X ← X−Y
            ENDWHILE
   WHILE Y≥0 DO X ← X+1
            Y ← Y−1
            ENDWHILE


Q   WHILE X≥0 DO X ← X−Y
            WHILE Y≥0 DO X ← X+1
                     Y ← Y−1
                     ENDWHILE
   ENDWHILE
```

For these program bodies, $DF(P) = 12$ while $DF(Q) = 15$ The only difference between P and Q is that in P the two loops are sequential, whereas in Q the loops are nested In P, therefore, the assignments to X and Y in the second loop can have no effect on their values in the first loop   In Q, however, the assignments to X and Y in the inner loop may affect their values in the outer loop

An obvious question is what kinds of syntactic modifications should leave the complexity of a program unchanged? That is, under what circumstances would one consider two programs to be as close as two programs can be syntactically? We propose that they have this relationship if they contain the same types of statements, in the same order, using the same variables and arithmetic operators Semantically, of course, the two programs may behave substantially differently on all or most of the elements of the domain Thus we shall say that P and Q are *almost identical* if P can be transformed into Q by applying the following transformation rules any number of times

(1) Replace a relational operator r_1 in a predicate in P with relational operator r_2

(2) Replace a constant c_1 in a predicate in P with constant c_2

(3) Replace a constant c_1 in an assignment statement in P with a constant c_2

PROPERTY 7 If P and Q are almost identical then $|P| = |Q|$

Clearly, this is a property which holds for the statement count, cyclomatic number, and data flow measures For the effort measure, however, this is not necessarily true, since, for example, the change of a relational operator might change the value of η_1 so that $\eta_1(P) \neq \eta_1(Q)$, while all other factors remain the same In such a case $E(P) \neq E(Q)$ Changes in constants might also change the value of η_2 and lead to a case for which $E(P) \neq E(Q)$

The last question we discuss is, given that the complexity of a program body should be no less than the complexities of each of its parts (Property 4), can we make a stronger statement? For example, should the complexity of a program body be no less than the sum of the complexities of its components? Intuitively, in order to implement a program, each of its parts must be implemented Thus one might want to require

PROPERTY $(\forall P)(\forall Q)(\ |P| + |Q| \leq |P,Q|\ )$

Since neither the effort measure nor data flow complexity fulfill Property 4, it follows immediately that they do not satisfy this property. From the relationships stated earlier, it follows that this property does hold for statement count (and data flow complexity if as a result of composing P and Q, two blocks are not merged into one.) Technically, this property *never* holds for cyclomatic number since for that measure, since $|P;Q| = |P|+|Q|-1 < |P|+|Q|$. But if cyclomatic number is changed so that

$$v' = e - n + 2p - 1 = \pi$$

then $|P;Q| = |P| + |Q|$, and this property holds. Note that the measure is not changed in any fundamental way by this modification, and thus we consider this property to hold for cyclomatic number. (Alternately, we could consider the modified property: $(\exists c)(\forall P)(\forall Q)(|P| + |Q| \leq |P;Q| + c)$ where c is a non-negative constant. Clearly with $c=1$, this modified property holds for cyclomatic number.)

But is this really what we want to require? Consider the program body P;P (that is, the same set of statements repeated twice.) Would it take twice as much time to implement or understand P;P as P? Probably not. In general, a measure which views the complexity of a program body as independent of its context (such as statement count or cyclomatic number) will satisfy this property. Although it seems reasonable that the complexity of a program body be related to the complexities of all of its parts, it is difficult to determine the precise desired relationship. We consider this an interesting open question.

We summarize our findings:

Property Number	Statement Count	Cyclomatic Number	Effort Measure	Data Flow Complexity
1	YES	YES	YES	YES
2	YES	YES	YES	YES
3	YES	NO	YES	NO
4	YES	YES	NO	NO
5	NO	NO	YES	YES
6	NO	NO	NO	YES
7	YES	YES	NO	YES

SUMMARY

We have introduced several properties which we believe a syntactic complexity measure should fulfill We have closely examined four proposed syntactic complexity measures to see which properties they have in common, and which properties distinguish them By viewing a program as an object built up from smaller programs, these important differences become clear Conceptually, both statement count and cyclomatic number view a program's components as having inherent complexity, regardless of their context in the program In contrast to this, the complexity of a program using the data flow measure depends directly on the placement of statements and how the components interact via the potential flow of data Programming effort falls somewhere between these two views A given group of statements will yield the same effort regardless of their order, but depending on the other program bodies with which a program body is composed to build a program, the amount that is contributed to the complexity by various textual units could vary

The failure to satisfy Property 3 is an important weakness of both the cyclomatic number and data flow measures The problem is that they rate too many programs as equally complex That is, they are not sensitive enough to what might reasonably be considered differences in program complexity

Even more fundamental, however, is the failure of the effort measure to satisfy Property 4 We believe it is so important that it calls into question its usefullness as a syntactic complexity measure, especially since $E(P)$ is supposed to directly predict the amount of time needed to implement P It is difficult to imagine how it is possible that it take longer to produce the initial part of a program, than the entire program

The data flow complexity measure also failed to satisfy Property 4, but in this case it is due to the fact that the measure only includes the flow of data between blocks, not within blocks Since two concatenated program bodies (or their parts) may form a single block, it is possible for the data flow complexity of P Q be less than that of P or Q Oviedo's assumption that it is easier to determine definition-reference relationships within blocks than between blocks seems reasonable But perhaps his conclusion that all intrablock data flow should be discounted is too strong Similarly, the assumption that multiple references to the same variable within a block add nothing to the complexity may also be too strong It seems likely that minor modifications of this measure can solve its failure to fulfill these properties

Properties 5-7 are desirable but much less fundamental than Properties 1-4 They point out subtle differences between programs that neither statement count nor cyclomatic number are responsive to They also identify positive aspects of using data flow to measure program complexity.

We have provided the foundation for comparing and evaluating software complexity measures in a formal way We have considered four of the most widely cited measures and have shown that there are substantial differences among them Hopefully, the properties proposed here can also serve as a foundation for the definition of new measures without the weaknesses of previously proposed measures

ACKNOWLEDGMENTS

I am grateful to Martin Davis, Phyllis Frankl, and Stewart Weiss for making many helpful and interesting suggestions

REFERENCES

[1] A L. Baker and S H Zweben, "A Comparison of Measures cf Control Flow Complexity," *IEEE Trans Software Eng* , Vol.SE-6, No.6, Nov 1980, pp 506-512

[2] M Blum, "On the Size of Machines," *Information and Control*, Vol 11, 1967, pp.257-265

[3] B Curtis, S.B Sheppard, P. Milliman, M A Borst, and T. Love, "Measuring the Psychological Complexity of Software Maintenance Tasks with the Halstead and McCabe Metrics," *IEEE Trans Software Eng* , Vol SE-5, No 2, March 1979, pp 96-104

[4] W M Evangelist, "Software Complexity Metric Sensitivity to Program Structuring Rules," *J Systems and Software*, Vol 3, 1983, pp 231-243

[5] R D Gordon, "Measuring Improvements in Program Clarity," *IEEE Trans Software Eng.*, Vol.SE-5, No 2, March 1979, pp.79-90

[6] M.H Halstead, *Elements of Software Science*, Elsevier North-Holland, New York, 1977

[7] W J Hansen, "Measurement of Program Complexity by the Pair (Cyclomatic Number, Operator Count," *SIGPLAN Notices*, Vol 13, No 3, March 1978, pp 29-33

[8] W Harrison and K Magel, "A Complexity Measure Based on Nesting Level," *ACM SIGPLAN Notices*, Mar 1981, pp 63-74

[9] M.S. Hecht, *Flow Analysis of Computer Programs*, North Holland, 1977

[10] P M Herman, "A Data Flow Analysis Approach to Program Testing," *Australian Computer J* , Vol 8, No 3, Nov 1976, pp 92-96.

[11] A Iannino, J D Musa, K Okumoto, and B Littlewood, "Criteria for Software Reliability Model Comparisons," *IEEE Trans Software Eng* , Vol SE-10, No 6, Nov 1984, pp 687-691

[12] S S Iyengar, N Parameswaran, and J Fuller, "A Measure of Logical Complexity of Programs," *Comput Lang.*, Vol.7, 1982, pp 147-160

[13] J L Knox and K C Tai, "An Empirical Evaluation of Program Complexity Metrics," Technical Report TR-84-06, North Carolina State Univ , 1984

[14] J W Laski and B Korel, "A Data Flow Oriented Program Testing Strategy," *IEEE Trans Software Eng* , Vol SE-9, No 3, May 1983, pp 347-354

[15] T J McCabe, "A Complexity Measure," *IEEE Trans Software Eng* , Vol SE-2, No 4, Dec 1976, pp 308-320

[16] G J Myers, "An Extension to the Cyclomatic Measure of Program Complexity," *SIGPLAN Notices*, Vol 12, No 10, Oct 1977, pp 61-64

[17] S C Ntafos, "On Required Element Testing," *IEEE Trans Software Eng* , Vol.SE-10, No 6, Nov 1984, pp 795-803

[18] E I Oviedo, "Control Flow, Data Flow and Program Complexity," *Proc IEEE COMPSAC*, Chicago, Ill , Nov 1980, pp 146-152

[19] P Piwowarski, "A Nesting Level Complexity Measure," *SIGPLAN Notices*, Vol 17, No 9, Sept 1982, pp 44-50

[20] S Rapps and E J Weyuker, "Data Flow Analysis Techniques for Program Test Data Selection," Dept of Computer Science Technical Rpt 023, Courant Institute of Mathematical Sciences, New York University, New York, Aug 1980

[21] S Rapps and E J. Weyuker, "Data Flow Analysis Techniques For Test Data Selection," *Proc 6th International Conference on Software Engineering*, Tokyo, Japan, September 1982, pp 272-278

[22] M Schaeffer, *A Mathematical Theory of Global Program Optimization*, Prentice-Hall, Englewood Cliffs, N J , 1973.

[23] T Sunohara, A Takano, K Uehara, and T Ohkawa, "Program Complexity Measure for Software Development Management," *Proc 5th International Conference on Software Engineering*, San Diego, March 1981, pp 100-106

[24] K-C Tai, "A Program Complexity Metric Based on Data Flow Information in Control Graphs," *Proc 7th International Conference on Software Engineering*, Orlando, Fla, March 1984, pp 239-248

[25] E J Weyuker, "The Applicability of Program Schema Results to Programs," *Int J Comput Inf Sci* , Vol 8, No 5, Nov 1979

[26] E J Weyuker, "Axiomatizing Software Test Data Adequacy," Computer Science Technical Report 99, Courant Institute of Mathematical Sciences, New York University, Jan 1983

[27] S N Woodfield, V Y Shen, and H E Dunsmore "A Study of Several Metrics for Programming Effort," *J Systems and Software*, Vol 2, 1981, pp 97-103

[28] M R Woodward, M A Hennell, and D Hedley, "A Measure of Control Flow Complexity in Program Text," *IEEE Trans Software Eng* , Vol SE-5, No 1, Jan 1979, pp 45-50

[29] S H Zweben and K-C Fung, "Exploring Software Science Relations in COBOL and APL," *Proc IEEE COMPSAC*, Chicago, Ill , Nov 1979, pp 702-707